I'M ALLERGIC

I'M ALLERGIC TO GRASS

D1508967

By Walter LaPlante

Gareth Stevens
PUBLISHING

Please visit our website, www.garethstevens.com. For a free color catalog of all our high-quality books, call toll free 1-800-542-2595 or fax 1-877-542-2596.

Library of Congress Cataloging-in-Publication Data

Names: LaPlante, Walter, author.
Title: I'm allergic to grass / Walter LaPlante.
Description: New York : Gareth Stevens Publishing, [2019] | Series: I'm allergic | Includes index.
Identifiers: LCCN 2018015059| ISBN 9781538229057 (library bound) | ISBN 9781538232408 (paperback) | ISBN 9781538232415 (6 pack)
Subjects: LCSH: Hay fever–Juvenile literature. | Hay fever in children–Juvenile literature. | Grasses–Juvenile literature. | Allergy in children–Juvenile literature.
Classification: LCC RC590 .L37 2019 | DDC 618.97/97–dc23
LC record available at https://lccn.loc.gov/2018015059

Published in 2019 by
Gareth Stevens Publishing
111 East 14th Street, Suite 349
New York, NY 10003

Copyright © 2019 Gareth Stevens Publishing

Designer: Laura Bowen
Editor: Kate Mikoley

Photo credits: cover, p. 1 Africa Studio/Shutterstock.com; p. 5 wavebreakmedia/Shutterstock.com; p. 7 ESB Basic/Shutterstock.com; p. 9 (timothy) Don Pedro28/Wikimedia Commons; p. 9 (Bermuda) Bidgee/Wikimedia Commons; p. 9 (rye) BotMultichill/Wikimedia Commons; p. 9 (Kentucky inset) Rasbak/Wikimedia Commons; p. 9 (Kentucky background) Rigel7/Wikimedia Commons; p. 11 CGN089/Shutterstock.com; p. 13 sirtravelalot/Shutterstock.com; p. 15 Kanghophoto/Shutterstock.com; p. 17 Rido/Shutterstock.com; p. 19 Jeff Greenough/Blend Images/Getty Images; p. 21 goodluz/Shutterstock.com.

Printed in the United States of America

CPSIA compliance information: Batch #CW19GS: For further information contact Gareth Stevens, New York, New York at 1-800-542-2595.

CONTENTS

Boldface words appear in the glossary.

The Springtime Blues

Achoo! Many people look forward to the sunny days of spring. But those allergic to grass don't! They're too busy sneezing. Grass allergies are one of the most common allergies. Allergies are the body **reacting** to something commonly harmless as if it's harmful.

A Pollen Problem

Sometimes grass allergies are called "hay fever." People allergic to grasses are **irritated** by **proteins** in grass pollen. Pollen is the yellow dust plants make that's carried to other plants. It's used to produce seeds. Pollen can float through the air for miles!

pollen

7

Grass Guess

There are hundreds of different kinds of grasses. Only some of them cause allergies. But, someone with grass allergies can be allergic to more than one type of grass. Which grasses cause allergy **symptoms** often has to do with where a person lives.

GRASSES THAT CAUSE ALLERGIES

timothy

Bermuda

rye

Kentucky

9

Where Do You Live?

In the northern parts of the United States, grasses **pollinate** in the spring and early summer. People with grass allergies have the worst symptoms then. In the southern parts of the United States, grasses pollinate all year. That makes having allergies worse!

Check Your Symptoms

The most common symptoms of grass pollen allergies are sneezing, watery eyes, and a runny nose. Your eyes, ears, and mouth might get **itchy**. People who have both **asthma** and grass allergies will likely cough more and may have trouble breathing.

Sometimes, a person with very bad grass allergies can get **hives**. A few people may get very sick if the proteins in the pollen get into their blood through a cut. They'll have trouble breathing and need a doctor's help.

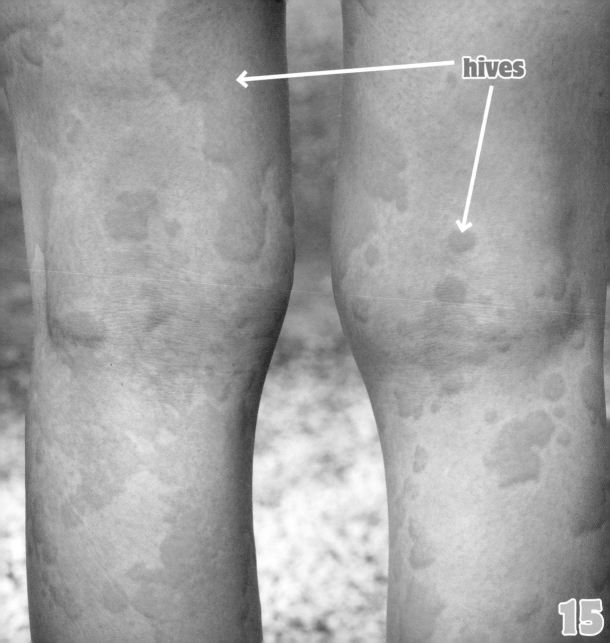

hives

15

Doctor's Orders

Even small amounts of grass pollen can cause allergic reactions. That's why if you think you have a grass allergy, you should get tested by your doctor. They can tell you what kinds of **medicines** to take that may help.

Allergies, Stay Away!

It's hard to stay away from grass pollen during some seasons. But, you can limit how much you're around it. Play inside on days the **forecast** says there will be a lot of pollen. Or, stay outside for shorter amounts of time.

Ask your parents to keep the grass in your yard short, and keep the windows closed when it gets mowed. Change your clothes when you come inside from playing in the grass. Most importantly, take the allergy medicine your doctor gives you!

GLOSSARY

asthma: a condition that makes it hard for a person to breathe

forecast: the informed guess about future weather that's often shown on TV or in newspapers

hives: a condition in which part of the skin becomes raised, red, and itchy

irritate: to make part of your body sore or painful

itchy: having an unpleasant feeling on your skin or inside your mouth or nose that makes you want to scratch

medicine: a drug taken to make a sick person well

pollinate: to take pollen from one flower, plant, or tree to another

protein: a necessary element found in all living things

react: to change after coming in contact with other matter

symptom: a sign that shows someone is sick

FOR MORE INFORMATION

BOOKS

Potts, Francesca. *All About Allergies*. Minneapolis, MN: Super Sandcastle, 2018.

Ribke, Simone T. *I Have Allergies*. New York, NY: Children's Press, 2016.

WEBSITES

All About Allergies
kidshealth.org/en/parents/allergy.html
Read about all kinds of allergies on this website.

Seasonal Allergies (Hay Fever)
kidshealth.org/en/parents/seasonal-allergies.html
Find out more about seasonal allergies here.

INDEX